The Via Dolorosa:
"Following Jesus in Jerusalem"

By Dr. Randall D. Smith

Introduction

For several years our students have asked us to make the notes of various lectures available in written form. This booklet is a part of a series created to respond to that request. The notes are from the teaching materials used in conjunction with the courses of study with Christian Travel Study Programs, Inc. This particular study is intended to give the reader a close-up view of the pilgrim's path known as the "Via Dolorosa" or to many as "The Way of Sorrows," and the journey to the Holy Sepulchre. For believers of every background, we have found that carefully recalling the suffering of Jesus in the Passion is a meaningful and often moving experience that helped the student of the New Testament grow in their faith and their love for their Savior.

The Via Dolorosa

Introduction

The route of the Via Dolorosa, marked by fourteen "stations" (reflection points), was created to be a "journey of reflection" that recalls the suffering of Jesus of Nazareth in the first century of the common era. The entire walk follows the pathway of just a few streets inside the Old City walls of Jerusalem, and can be completed in a little more than an hour. Yet, the walk was not intended to be taken hastily, as it follows a story from the Gospel accounts that is powerful and dramatic, and deserves some time for pondering along the way. The end of this journey is within the incense darkened stone walls of Church of the Holy Sepulchre, a central place of pilgrimage to many believers celebrating the place of the resurrection of Jesus since at least the fourth century. The sites along the route are certainly significant for the Christian pilgrim, but they also add unique historical treasures to the dynamic texture of the city of Jerusalem.

The general route marks out places to recall the Gospel recorded events from the condemnation of Jesus by Pontius Pilate to the place of Jesus' execution, and the locus where His body was placed in the tomb of Joseph of Arimithea. As a pilgrim makes their way along the route, each station is deliberately marked on or beside the stone roadway. These were *chosen* sites, based on the desire of Christians to reflect along the trail of sufferings of Jesus and were not intended (in many cases) to mark "the actual spot" where ancient events occurred. One Catholic scholar has said "the Via Dolorosa is defined by faith, not by history". [1]

The Latin terms "Via Dolorosa" emphasize the brutal sufferings of the Savior for the Christian – an ever present reminder of the cost of His payment for the sins of man. The cobbled streets follow the route between what scholars believe was the ancient

---

[1] O'Connor, Fr. Jerome, The Holy Land (Oxford: Oxford University Press, 1986), p. 33.

The Via Dolorosa: Following Jesus in Jerusalem

location of the Antonia Fortress of the Herodian period (one possible place of temporary residence for the Roman governor Pontius Pilate) to the Church of the Holy Sepulchre (a long held site for the hill of Golgotha).

The actual place where Pontius Pilate stayed during the events detailed in the Gospel of John 19 is not known. Though every detail of the life and journeys of Jesus have been carefully studied over the generations, significant scholarly debate has left the identification of the *Praetorium*, or "place of judgment," a mystery. The New Testament reflects that Pilate was visiting the city during the last week of Jesus' ministry, but only offers hints as to His exact location. Pontius Pilate resided mainly in Caesarea but came up to Jerusalem during the Passover feast. Because the time of Passover was a time when Messianic expectations were characteristically at their highest, this was the time when Pontius Pilate would need to be in Jerusalem watching over the city.

For a clue to where the governor may have been, some suggest we search the writings of Roman historians. In Philo's writings, specifically the "*Delegation to Gaias*" (no. 38), he suggested that Pilate normally went to the palace of Herod, the remains of which can now be seen inside the Jaffa Gate of Jerusalem, south of the Citadel. Philo suggested this was a place to adjudicate matters remanded to the governor and also an excellent place to watch over the city when a stirring began. The historian Josephus mentioned that one of Pilate's successors, Governor Florus, stayed at that same palace and that he had a raised platform in front of the building where he would sit as people presented themselves before the tribunal. This sounds suspiciously like "Gabbatha" or the "Lithostratos" – the raised platform mentioned in the trial of Jesus (John 19:13). Despite these evidences, the current route was chosen which presumed Pilate's place at the *Antonia*, a Roman fortress located north of the ancient Temple Mount. Though weaker in historical documentation, the choice was not without merit if one takes into account the possibility of an armed uprising that could easily have occurred at that moment in history.

The Via Dolorosa: Following Jesus in Jerusalem

In fact, the choice of the Antonia Fortress site as the location of Pilate's ad-hoc court was made for several reasons. This fortress also appears to have been built on a large foundational platform of paving stones (like the other western hill palace complex). More recent excavations have demonstrated the pavement under the "Chapel of the Condemnation" and the "Ecce Homo Convent" to be from the Roman period. It seems clear the pavement was placed in its current position after the time of Jesus by the reconstruction of Emperor Hadrian, but there are indications that it was cut originally for use earlier. Hence, the Antonia appears to have had a large paved courtyard that was a somewhat larger area than the other palace (inside Jaffa Gate). In addition to its size, the proximity to the ancient Temple area made it a particularly helpful vantage-point for the Roman governor concerned about insurrection during this festival. The palace at Jaffa gate was well fortified, but offered little view of the happenings at the time of the Passover. The Antonia is clearly the fortress referred to in the Book of Acts in the scene of the arrest of the Apostle Paul. [2]

The tradition of observing reflection along a path in "stations" of suffering (now referred to as the "Stations of the Cross") began in earnest in the Byzantine period, but had an earlier root. Think about that root for a moment. Because of the vast size of the Roman Empire that grew from the 3rd century BCE until its dissection in the west in 476 CE, the Empire needed methods to build cohesion among all its citizenry. After all, with an empire stretching from Scotland to the Saudi desert, with vast numbers of people groups that had no singular alphabet (let alone tradition), it was essential to build the singular communal identity as a "Roman". One way this was readily accomplished was by the use of "spectacles", while another was the "standardization" of the Roman city. In each Roman city, careful

---

[2] Acts 21:37, where the Greek word "parembolaen" was used as barracks, fortress or military encampment. The location clearly denotes the Antonia as Paul was being taken up a stairway adjacent to the Temple compound.

attempts to follow a familiar design were made, so one felt a part of the empire no matter where you traveled.

One of the standard operations of a Roman city was that of the "Vigiles" or night watchmen and fire brigades. These torch-bearing men walked the streets of each city at night, patrolling with a watchful eye. They stopped regularly at prescribed "stations" that were marked in the street to call out the watch by saying: "Third watch of the night, all clear!" Thus, the stations were markers to guarantee specific routes were always watched.

Generations later, sometime in the 6th century (CE), on "Holy Thursday" (the Thursday of the week that annually recalls the events of the Passion of Jesus), Byzantine pilgrims went from Gethsemane to Calvary in a reflective journey along their own chosen route. In the 7th and 8th centuries, various readings from the Gospels were added to the reflective prayers along the route to supplement the experience and make the walk even more meaningful. The route for those pilgrims who came in the 8th century probably started from Gethsemane, went around the city south to Mount Zion to remember events from the questioning of Jesus by Jewish authorities at the "house of Joseph Caiaphas", and eventually ended in the Church of the Holy Sepulchre via a route from the south of the city.

Under Islamic authorities, the Christian pilgrim experience was halted for a time, and not well documented when it did occur. During the Crusader period (1099-1187 CE) essentially two different walks were observed. Western and Eastern Christians observed two different routes based on the location in which they possessed property marking their holy shrines, either on the western hill of Jerusalem or on the eastern hill. Those (primarily Western or Latin Christians) who possessed properties designated "holy places" on the eastern hill believed that the Praetorium referred to in the New Testament was north of the Temple Mount. That route ran along a similar line of streets to what the Via Dolorosa is today. Other Eastern or Orthodox Christians who possession of "holy places" on the western hill (called by that time "Mount Zion") along with shrines on the upper ridge inside the Armenian and Christian quarters. They felt the route was best recalled passing from the house of Caiaphas (now the Armenian property atop Mt. Zion opposite the Zion Gate of the Old City) heading north through the Armenian and Christian quarters to the Church of the Holy Sepulchre.

By the 14th century, friars from the Franciscan order of the Catholic church began to organize a procession in the steps of Jesus through the "Passion Week" (the week recalling the events of Jesus' suffering, death and resurrection) for Christian pilgrims to make their journey to the land more spiritually meaningful. Pilgrim records indicate the starting point, however, was within the Church of the Holy Sepulchre – a route that remained throughout the 14th and 15th centuries. This focused on themes in the torment of Christ, and not chronology of the story. Within the next one hundred years, some European pilgrims began to make pictured representations of various stations or reflective places in their home churches in Europe. These "Stations of the Cross" began to make appearances in the art of the pre-Renaissance period, and the motifs were well established by the period of the Italian Renaissance artists.

At the same time, Eastern Christians, (both residents and visitors in Jerusalem) tended to recall eight (or so) stations. The Western (Latin) Christians then eventually added several traditions to make up the 14 stations. The added stories took hold and eventually the Western European tradition became the norm for recalling the sufferings of Jesus. The actual route of the Stations of the Cross as we have them was fixed by the 18th century, but the number of stations only became "fixed" in the 19th century – all relatively recent.

The current route of the Via Dolorosa, extends from the Chapel of the Flagellation and the El Omariyeh School to its ending at the place marked for ancient "Golgotha", some 1,700-meters away. The first nine "Stations of the Cross" are located along the route itself and the last five are located within the Church of the Holy Sepulchre (following the Western European traditions and route). Because of this, many of the sites along the Via Dolorosa belong to, or are overseen by the Latin Catholic Order of St.

The Via Dolorosa: Following Jesus in Jerusalem

Francis (Franciscans). Franciscan monks have been in Jerusalem since the 13th century. Their Order was founded in 1212 and primarily focused on the poor, the sick and needy. It is the largest of the Catholic Orders and the order became the custodian of most of the "holy sites" in the land (now referred to as "Terra Sancta" properties). Each Friday afternoon at 3:00 pm the Franciscans lead the walk for pilgrims to retrace the Via Dolorosa and lead prayers in each of the 14 stations.

The Stations

There are fourteen stations recalled today, each to represent either a New Testament event, or a meaningful addition to the story to help join an important theme to those events. After the stations below, if the event is referenced in the Gospels, the verses are included parenthetically to help a pilgrim identify the event within the text.

Station I: Jesus was condemned to death (Mk. 15:16; Jn. 19:13).

Mark 15:16-20 "The soldiers took Him away into the palace (that is, the Praetorium), and they called together the whole [Roman] cohort. 17 They dressed Him up in purple, and after twisting a crown of thorns, they put it on Him; 18 and they began to acclaim Him, "Hail, King of the Jews!" 19 They kept beating His head with a reed, and spitting on Him, and kneeling and bowing before Him. 20 After they had mocked Him, they took the purple robe off Him and put His [own] garments on Him. And they led Him out to crucify Him."

The first station is actually located inside the El Omariyeh Boys School compound on the north side of the "Haram esh-Sharif" at the site of the meeting between the ancient Temple courtyard and the approximate location of the *Antonia Fortress*. Excavations of the fortress area have yielded only slight remains, and the exact size and shape of the fortress is not certain, but part of the escarpment is exposed on the south (facing the Dome of the

Rock). The Roman historian Josephus speaks of an incredible fortification built by Herod the Great in about the year 35 BCE, on the site of a previous smaller Hasmonean barracks.[3] A rock cut pool called the "Struthion Pool" was apparently adjacent to the fort and can be viewed below the Convent of the Sisters of Zion at Ecce Homo, between Station II and III. Some understand the comments of Josephus to infer that a Roman assault ramp was built above the pool to enter and sack the fortress after Zealots had taken control of it in the First Revolt. It may be from this location the Romans entered onto the Temple complex, destroying brigades of Jewish defenders. The pool was eventually covered by Hadrian in the establishment of "Aelia Capitolina".

As mentioned in the introduction above, some scholars believe that the *Praetorium*, mentioned in John's Gospel may have been the Antonia Fortress. The text describes "a place that is called the pavement" (John 19:13). Various excavations have revealed parts of the Roman structures of the area and a large pavement was partially uncovered in the vicinity. Recent excavations indicate its position (above the Struthion pool) indicates a proper date as the second century CE, but others insist it was in secondary use from an earlier pavement of the *Antonia Fortress*. Secondary use of such large fitted paving stones by the Romans was not rare.

The first station at the school is located in a structure that was originally built by King Issa Hanafia in the year 1217, on the north edge of the ancient Temple Mount. An earlier Crusader period "Chapel of Repose" was apparently dismantled on the site, and the "madrasa" (Islamic school) was built. Expanded in the fourteenth century, the aged building was completely redesigned by the Turks in 1838. Stone from a monastery that was once attached to St. Anne's was used to build a barracks for the Turkish army. The school was supplanted by the Turkish

---

[3] See War 5:238-47. The previous "Baris" fortress was apparently entirely redesigned and expanded, but scholars suspect Josephus of exaggeration in the description of the Herodian fort.

army for part of the nineteenth century, but was eventually restored to its educational function in 1923, and is now a boy's school with a lovely open courtyard.

In the excavation of the El Omariyeh school area an inscribed stone plaque from the period of the Second Temple was uncovered. This was a stone marker that prohibited strangers and non-Jews from entering the inner court of the Temple. It is one of two such inscriptions found showing that the "wall of partition" was a physical wall in the Temple area.[4] The inscription was transported to the Istanbul Museum for display.

Station II: Jesus received the cross (John 19:1-3).

John 19:1 Pilate then took Jesus and scourged Him. 2 And the soldiers twisted together a crown of thorns and put it on His head, and put a purple robe on Him; 3 and they [began] to come up to Him and say, "Hail, King of the Jews!" and to give Him slaps [in the face].

The second station is also located within the confines of the former *Antonia Fortress*. Directly across from the El Omariyeh school is the Franciscan Monastery of the Flagellation. Within the compound are two important shrines: *The Chapel of the Flagellation* and *The Chapel of the Condemnation*. Between the two chapels a sunlit courtyard offers a place for pilgrims to rest on a bench away from the busy street.

The domed eastern chapel recalls the "crown of thorns" that Jesus received at the *Praetorium* (Mark 15:17, John 18:28). Pilate had Jesus scourged and handed Him over to be crucified from the site of the *Praetorium* (John 19:1 and 19:16). Today the chapel is called the *Chapel of the Condemnation.* It was erected

---

[4] The Apostle Paul was accused of taking a non-Jew into the inner court of the Temple, and was arrested for this infraction (though not guilty). Acts 21 records that Paul had been seen in town with non-Jews, and when he showed up at the Temple, there was an inference that he brought his companions along. Paul also referred to the "wall of partition" as symbolically destroyed in the death of Jesus, cp. Eph. 2:14.

shortly after the Franciscans purchased the property in 1903. During the construction the remains of a mosque were discovered. Below the mosque had been built over two earlier structures - a Byzantine church, and part of the large second century "Hadrianic" pavement. The large pavement stones, some of which show groves and games cut into them just as on many Roman pavements, make up the floor of the Chapel. The modern buildings, which are part of the compound, contain a library and a large archeology museum.

Directly across from the *Chapel of the Condemnation*, within the same compound, is the *Chapel of the Flagellation*. The original structure was a medieval church that was later destroyed. Rebuilt in 1839, the site recalls the flogging of Jesus on a pavement (Greek: *lithostrotos*) thought to be near there (Mark 15:15 and John 19:1). The 1839 chapel was later torn down and was rebuilt in 1927-9 by Antonio Barluzzi who was inspired by 12th century architecture. Beautiful stained glass windows, which are the work of L. Picchiarini and D. Cambelotti depict the flogging of Jesus, the washing of the hands, and the triumph of Barabbas. Pilgrim stories from the Crusader period mention the area was a collapsed stable and tell of a Moslem woman that brought Christian pilgrims in to "hear the cries of those who persecuted Jesus" for a small sum. No remains of these buildings have survived except what Barluzzi reused in the current chapel.

Above the street and further along in the walk, between stations II and III, you will pass underneath the ancient arch of the Sisters of Zion Convent, the "*Ecce Homo Arch*." This was once thought to be the place where Pontius Pilate presented Jesus to the crowds: "*Ecce Homo*," or "Behold the Man" (John 19:5). The arch has been more recently dated, however. Some scholars argue for a date close to the time of Jesus [5] but most accept a second century (Hadrianic period) date.

---

[5] O'Connor, p. 32.

Station III: Jesus fell the first time.

At the end of the street, the Via Dolorosa curves south joining Tariq El-Wad Street (also called HaGai Street) for a short time. This main thoroughfare follows the bottom of the Tyropoean Valley that cuts through the middle of the Old City from the Damascus Gate in the north, to the Dung Gate in the south. Across from the Austrian Hospice, along this short piece of the Via Dolorosa that is shared in common with el-Wad, a small chapel the marks the third station.

The Gospels do not make mention of Jesus falling under the weight of the cross. However, the station was added to emphasize the humanity of Christ – suffering and exhausted. The front of the chapel was built into a structure that was originally a 15th century entrance to the Hamam Es Sultan Turkish baths. The three fanciful pointed arches are blocked now, but were a porch or vestibule to the original bathhouse. In 1856 the Armenian Catholics purchased the property that led to the baths, which by this time were no longer in use, and built a chapel. A 1947-8 renovation of the chapel was financed by a collection taken up by the Polish army during and after the Second World War. Their gift was the adorning of the chapel doorway with a sculptured pediment by A. Minghetti. The entry area, now closed off with an iron railing contains a simple column marker, a part of the column that tradition holds was next to the place Jesus fell.. The pediment relief above the entrance, *"Jesus Falls Under the Cross"*, is based on another work of art by Thaddeus Zielinsky.

Station IV: Jesus was seen by His afflicted mother.

Past the blocked doorway and column marker is an opening to a courtyard of the Armenian Catholic Patriarchate. The adjacent chapel, accessed also from this doorway, leads to the "Church of Our Lady of the Spasm". The chapel borders the fourth station, located just about 10 meters further south on el-Wad Street.

The *Chapel of Our Lady of the Spasm*, which recalls the sorrow of the Virgin Mary, is still a place of pilgrimage to women who have lost a child. When the construction on the chapel began in 1881, foundation holes yielded a number of evidences that an earlier Byzantine chapel was beneath. Mosaic tiles were discovered, and eventually a floor was exposed. The mosaic depicts a set of footprints, which were interpreted by some to represent the sandals of Mary. Felix Fabri, a Dominican priest and pilgrim of the fifteenth century saw a ruin there that he termed "The Church of St. Mary of the Swoon". The adorned entry at Station IV is also a sculpted pediment. The door below actually accesses the side of the chapel, the front is open to the courtyard inside.

Though a small part of the chapel was also built over the southern portion of the Hamam Es Sultan Turkish baths, a story was related as early as Crusader times that the area was holy and could not be built upon. The tradition passed to Fr. Fabri was that anyone attempting to build on the site saw their project destroyed before they could complete it. He also reported that no one was permitted to remove stones from the rubble of the former chapel.

Though not mentioned in the Gospels as present at the questionings of Jesus, the Virgin Mary was present at the Crucifixion according to the account in the Gospel of John (see Jn. 19:26-27). There is little doubt that the appearance of Jesus on the way to the cross was shocking and gruesome to behold. The tradition developed that Mary followed Jesus through the alleys on the way to the cross agonizing and crying aloud, a state of loud mourning not uncommon in burials of the Near East even today. At the first site of her afflicted and beaten Son, one tradition states that she was overcome with grief and fainted.

The value of including such a tradition is that even the modern pilgrim can understand the human setting of the redemption of man. The blood of Jesus was shed for sin, but this is theoretical and theological. On this street in Jerusalem, a mother's heart was broken. This simple human story tugs the heart of any mother who has watched their child suffer, an unspeakable anguish of the soul is remembered here.

Station V: Simon took up the Cross (Mark 15:21).

Mark 15:20b "...And they led Him out to crucify Him. 21 They pressed into service a passer-by coming from the country, Simon of Cyrene (the father of Alexander and Rufus), to bear His cross."

The fifth station is located about twenty meters further south on Tariq el-Wad Street, at the southwest corner of the intersection. The Franciscans purchased the site in about 1850, and later built a small oratory in 1895. The exterior door is prominently marked with a Roman numeral "V". The oratory was created for a reflection place to recall the day when Simon the Cyrene was compelled to carry the cross (Mark 15:21 and Luke 23:26).

A bystander to the events of Jesus' punishing walk to the city gate, Simon was thrust into the street and given the cross beam of the cross to carry for Jesus. He may have been visiting the city for the Passover from his home country (probably modern Libya). We have little information about Simon today, probably because his family was known to the first century Christians, and the writers felt no need to elaborate. The writer of the Gospel if Mark did tell us of his sons, Rufus and Alexander (Mk. 15:21), probably leaders or prominent followers in the early church.

The story was specifically cited in this memorial walk to help pilgrims reflect on the terrible injustice in the whole scene. Jesus was summarily condemned, and that without just cause. In addition, an unrelated and uncharged man is thrust into the unjust punishment to participate against his will. The inhumanity of man and his hard-hearted injustice are no more clearly seen than in this description. It is a worthy remembrance on the way to Calvary's redemption scene.

Station VI: Veronica wiped the face of Jesus.

The sixth station is located halfway up the hill between the fifth and seventh stations. The Greek Catholic (Melkite) "Chapel of the Holy Face" recalls the tradition of the compassionate act of a woman wiping the face of Jesus. The door is marked with the station number at the traditional house of Veronica.

The tradition of Veronica is that of a woman wiping the face of Jesus with her veil so that the veil took on itself the image of the face of Jesus. The image on the veil was reportedly responsible for a number of miracles and has been kept at St. Peter's Basilica in Rome since the year 707* (This date is uncertain, but is widely accepted).

The chapel was built in 1882 and belongs to the Order of Little Sisters of Jesus. During construction of the chapel, remains of what were apparently the edges of two monasteries were discovered. The larger section was the Monastery of St. Cosmas, which is known to have existed in Jerusalem between the years 546 and 563. Part of the chapel also falls over the edge of what appears to be remains from the Monastery of St. Damian. The original 1882 chapel was completely restored in 1953 by Antonio Barlutzi. He completely refashioned the altar in the renovation.

It is worth noting that *"vera"* is the Latin term for "face," and *"icona"* the term for "image." *Vera-icona* likely evolved in the tradition to Veronica – the name of the woman. It originates from *"the face image,"* referring to the image on the veil.

Station VII: Jesus fell a second time.

Rising to a high point on the street at the intersection with Khan ez-Zeit Street (Olive Oil Market Street), pilgrims see a small marker outside of a Franciscan chapel which recalls Jesus falling a second time. This bustling center is built along the axis of the main street of Byzantine Jerusalem ("cardo").

Originally there were two chapels built in 1875 behind the door that marks the seventh station. One chapel was built above the other and connected by stairs. The lower chapel contained a capital of the "Cardo" (main street) of Byzantine Jerusalem.

The area became known as the *Gate of Judgment*, because of the tradition of death notices being hung on the edge of a city wall as prisoners were marched out to the area of crucifixion outside of the city. This was a common practice during the middle ages in a number of European cities and some felt that perhaps it had happened in the case of Jesus as well. Though the column is of a later street, the seventh station may well roughly mark the edge of the wall and the area of the so-called "Gate of Judgment".

The second fall, also not a part of the New Testament record, reminds the pilgrim of the frail body of the tortured Jesus. The physical reality of His suffering is illustrated in the weakness of his body.

Station VIII: Jesus spoke to the daughters of Jerusalem (Luke 23:27).

Luke 23: 27 And following Him was a large crowd of the people, and of women who were mourning and lamenting Him. 28 But Jesus turning to them said, "Daughters of Jerusalem, stop weeping for Me, but weep for yourselves and for your children. 29 "For behold, the days are coming when they will say, Blessed are the barren, and the wombs that never bore, and the breasts that never nursed.' 30 "Then they will begin TO SAY TO THE MOUNTAINS, 'FALL ON US,' AND TO THE HILLS, 'COVER US.' 31 "For if they do these things when the tree is green, what will happen when it is dry?"

Standing in front of the Seventh Station, pilgrims observe an alley like street left of the door to the chapel, heading south from Khan ez-Zeit Street. Just sixteen steps up the alley the street leads to a round marker embedded on the left wall at the eighth station: "Jesus speaks to the daughters of Jerusalem". The small

Latin cross on the marker is etched into the bottom of a column inserted in the wall of the Greek Orthodox Convent of St. Caralambos. Along the top of the cross are the letters representing the name of Jesus Christ (ICXC), and the letters *NIKA* appear beside the cross. These letters (*NIKA*) form the word for "victory", and should be coupled to read "Jesus Christ is victorious!"

The speaking to the daughters is recorded in Luke 23:27-28.

Station IX: Jesus fell a third time.

The ninth station is the last station outside of the Church of the Holy Sepulchre. The column marker is up 28 steps at the Coptic Church on the corner before you turn into the Holy Sepulchre itself.

A door leads into the crypt of the Holy Sepulchre and the backside of the church of St. Helena, the Chapel of the True Cross. The cannons of the Church of the Holy Sepulchre used to have their living quarters in that area during the Crusader period and in the courtyard that is inhabited by the Abyssinian monks today.

Station X: Jesus was stripped of His garments (John 19:23-24).

John 19:23 "Then the soldiers, when they had crucified Jesus, took His outer garments and made four parts, a part to every soldier and [also] the tunic; now the tunic was seamless, woven in one piece. 24 So they said to one another, "Let us not tear it, but cast lots for it, [to decide] whose it shall be"; [this was] to fulfill the Scripture: "THEY DIVIDED MY OUTER GARMENTS AMONG THEM, AND FOR MY CLOTHING THEY CAST LOTS."

Near to the stairway at the main entrance of the Holy Sepulchre is place where the stripping of Jesus' garments is remembered.

There is a small entry to a chapel at the top of the stairs located outside the main door, although it is now closed to the general public.

The event of the stripping of Jesus is part of the New Testament record as the casting of lots for the vesture of Jesus is mentioned (John 19:23-24).

The typical garments worn in this period would have certainly included: a headdress, thought by most scholars to resemble the turban wrapping associated with India and Pakistan today; sandals for the feet; a tunic that covered the body to the feet; and an overcoat with a belt. Some ancient sources disclose that a wrap undergarment was also worn, but this would have been discarded by the executioners. The Gospel writer gives the detail that that there were four parts distributed to four soldiers, but the top coat, made without seam in the case of Jesus, was given to the soldier upon whom the fortunes of the lots fell (John 19:23-4).

Station XI: Jesus was nailed to the cross (John 19:18).

John 19:18 "There they crucified Him, and with Him two other men, one on either side, and Jesus in between."

Inside the front door of the church, which now faces to the south (the original church entry was to the east), there is a set of steep stone stairs that must be ascended to arrive at the eleventh station.

The chapel is Roman Catholic and has a detailed mosaic affixed to the eastern wall which reminds pilgrims of the nailing of Jesus onto the cross. The style of the cross depicted in the mosaic was determined by a European artist and probably has little, if any, resemblance to the actual event. Nevertheless, the purpose of such artwork, like church icons, is to help set an atmosphere for prayer and remembrance.

The most helpful and clear archeological evidence of crucifixion of the Roman period in the ancient province of Judea is that of "the case of the crucified man" discovered in a burial site in greater Jerusalem's Giv'at HaMivtar area. The discovery was found in a tomb which was unexpectedly uncovered by road and construction work in the 1960s. An emergency excavation of the tomb yielded a number of ossuaries, boxes containing the bones of the dead, which were carefully examined by archeologists. Much can be learned from the remains – food deficiencies, the presence of certain diseases in the long dead, ages and physical descriptions of the people contained in the tomb. In a way, such a burial "speaks" to the archaeologist and historian alike.

One of the ossuaries contained a curiosity that is still the subject of much discussion (See *Israel Exploration Journal*, vol.35, no.1, 1985, pp. 22-7). The excavator, Vasilios Tzaferis, examined the skeletal remains of a male who appeared to have been crucified at about the age of 28. Evidence for the man's death by crucifixion included a bent nail, still positioned in the foot bones. The nail was 11.5 cm (4.5 inches) in length. When the family buried the remains of this man, they appear to have been unable to remove the nail, so it was buried with him.

Tests were run on the remains and on the nail both by Nico Haas of Hebrew University Hadassah Medical School and subsequently by Joseph Zias, an anthropologist with the Israel Exploration Society along with Eliezer Sekeles, a colleague of Haas at the University Medical School. It was determined that the crucifixion in this particular case did not include the use of the *crucibellum* (a sledgehammer) that was sometimes used to break the legs of the crucified victim. Further, the victim did not appear to have evidence of hand injury, implying that his arms were roped and not nailed, and may have been nailed to an olive tree. The evidence of olive wood's use below the nail head, as a plaque to stop the nail from pulling through the foot, and the suggestion by Tzaferis that the crucifixion was on an olive tree would indicate that the man was positioned on a low cross. If the same type of crucifixion were applied to the Gospel narrative,

Jesus may well have been nailed to a crossbeam (*patibulum*) and then boosted onto a small olive tree with his legs bent. Despite the church artists who depict Him on a high cross, that me be a less accurate picture of the original horrifying execution.

Station XII: Jesus died on the cross (John 19:30).

John 19:28 After this, Jesus, knowing that all things had already been accomplished, to fulfill the Scripture, said, "I am thirsty." 29 A jar full of sour wine was standing there; so they put a sponge full of the sour wine upon [a branch] [of] hyssop and brought it up to His mouth. 30 Therefore when Jesus had received the sour wine, He said, "It is finished!" And He bowed His head and gave up His spirit.

Before reaching the twelfth station, notice on the eastern wall, to the left of the mosaic of the eleventh station, the statue of the Virgin Mary with a dagger placed to wound her heart. This painful expression of her face was first sculpted in wood in the 16th century and then coated to give the smooth look to her facial skin and hands. The icon was brought as a gift from Lisbon in 1778, and is part of a small altar of reflection for the pilgrim to recall the painful journey from the perspective of Mary – a theme begun in station IV. The subject of the art refers to Luke 2:34-5 in the prophecy that "A sword will pierce your (Mary's) heart." Of all who could witness the cross, no one would see it through the eyes of Jesus' mother. Hers was a unique pain felt by parents who have lost a child; those who saw their child taken from before their own eyes.

The death of Jesus on the cross is graphically depicted behind the Greek altar which was placed above a piece of the bedrock of Calvary (also *Golgotha*, John 19:17). Below the altar, pilgrims frequently bow down and reach into a small dark hole to touch the surface of the now well-worn bedrock of Calvary. The significance of the touch for many is that the place marks in Christian memory, if not in fact, the place where the blood of Jesus spilled onto the earth. It is that blood, Christians believe, that takes away the sin of man. The death of Jesus for the satisfaction of the rebellion of man against his Creator is at the heart of the Gospel.

This room is a mixture of gold and gore, splendor and spilled blood – for it is the central fixture to the Gospel – that men can have their sin and rebellion erased by allowing the payment of the Savior to wash away the stain before God, and make them new. It is the heart of the "Good News" (Gospel).

Station XIII: Jesus was taken down from the cross (Luke 23:53).

Luke 23:53 "And he took it down and wrapped it in a linen cloth, and laid Him in a tomb cut into the rock, where no one had ever lain."

Below the terrace of stations XI and XII, in the open area near the entrance of the Church of the Holy Sepulchre is a station to recall the body of Jesus taken down from the cross and prepared for burial (Luke 23:53). A large and colorful mosaic has more recently been added to the wall of the area to depict the scene of the removal from the cross and the preparation of the body on a slab of stone. Such preparations were made in some parts of the Mediterranean in antiquity, but do not conform to Jewish custom, which made preparations inside the rock-cut tomb for reasons of privacy. Yet, the tradition was made by those from other places, and they come now to wipe the stone, then kiss the place – to pay homage to the One placed there long ago. It is a place of worship for One broken on their behalf.

Below the mosaic, positioned on the floor, this mere slab of stone recalls a preparation table. If the idea is unclear, it graphically appears on the mosaic. It is still a moving site to watch pilgrims from all parts of the world, washing the now smoothed stone and then gently kissing it, reflecting on the body of Jesus that was broken for them.

Station XIV: Jesus was placed in the tomb (Matthew 27:60).

Matthew 27:57 "When it was evening, there came a rich man from Arimathea, named Joseph, who himself had also become a disciple of Jesus. 58 This man went to Pilate and asked for the body of Jesus. Then Pilate ordered it to be given [to him]. 59 And Joseph took the body and wrapped it in a clean linen cloth, 60 and laid it in his own new tomb, which he had hewn out in the rock; and he rolled a large stone against the entrance of the tomb and went away."

Inside the Chapel of the Angel, a small door leads into the place marking the original tomb. Though the stone of the original cliff has long since been quarried away, the room recalls the geographical location, and has been the central site of the Christian pilgrimage experience for generations.

The Gospel writer recorded the tomb was that of Joseph of Arimathea (probably modern Rama), and that it was a new tomb in that it had not been used before (Matthew 27:59). We can also read that the tomb was in a garden (or grove) setting and had it was sealed by a rolling stone (Mark 15:43-6, Luke 23:50, John 19:41).

The station at the tomb is recalled at the entrance to the first of two antechambers, at the door of the Chapel of the Angel, reminding the pilgrim of the great words of hope from the angel, "He is not here, He is risen as He said!" (Mark 16:6). The remarkable words reminded that in the Gospel message, the Savior's death was accepted by God as sufficient payment for sin, and publicly endorsed in the resurrection from the dead.

The message of the Savior is not that He died, but rather that He died and the payment was accepted – and He has RISEN!

The History of the Church of the Holy Sepulchre

This central shrine of Christianity through the ages has been described as dark, cramped and cold by many; and yet it offers a view of what most archeological scholars would say is an authentic site for the crucifixion and resurrection. Fr. O'Conner describes it best when he writes, "The frailty of man is nowhere more apparent than here, it epitomizes the human condition. The empty who come to be filled will leave desolate" (*The Holy Land: An Archeological guide from 1700 to Present*, pp. 43). The words sting, but thankfully were written more than ten years ago, before the new renovations to the church which are lightening the color and adding new life to the formerly dreary look.

The names of the structures that form the church compound have evolved over the centuries, with various sources using any or all of the following terms: the *Martyrion*, the *Holy Sepulchre*, the *Anastasis*, and the *edicule*. The *Martyrion* refers to the first church (4th century) which was built on the site, and means "the place of witness." The more commonly used term, the *Holy Sepulchre*, refers to the medieval church now at the site of the *Martyrion*, and incorporates many earlier elements of the site. The sepulchre, or tomb, is that of the Resurrection and is commonly referred to as the *Anastasis*. The building over the place of the former tomb is also referred to as the *edicule*.

The Biblical terminology for the site includes the terms *Golgotha*, the Aramaic word for "skull," and *Calvary*, from the Latin term *calvaria* also meaning "skull" (Matthew 27:33, Luke 23:33, John 19:17).

The actual history of the site began in about the 9th or 8th century BCE, when the area was used as a quarry because of its high quality meleke cenomanian limestone. Some scholars have speculated that the origins of the quarry may be later, at the time of the building of the new defenses for the city of Jerusalem under King Hezekiah in preparation for the coming Assyrian invasion. The quarry was cut in the east to a deeper level and stretched north and east, but left an outcrop of rock in the southwest side, possibly because of the lateral cracks in the stone. The rock outcropping was left standing in the quarry and is now the platform that recalls the place of the crucifixion.

By the end the 1st century BCE, tombs were cut into the cliff sides of the former quarry. One small tomb exists today and is clearly a *kokhim* style tomb (niches) which was characteristic of tombs in Jerusalem between 50 BCE and 70CE. The tombs and alleged execution site become important by about 30CE, when Jesus was crucified and buried nearby. The New Testament places the Resurrection in a garden setting, at a tomb near to the place of the cross (John 19).

Between 41 and 44CE, Herod Agrippa I laid the foundation of a wall commonly referred to as the *Third Wall*. The new wall, which was not completed until 66CE, expanded the city on the north side and thereby included the site of the quarry and old tombs within the city limits.

By 135 CE, after the second Jewish revolt had ended, Hadrian replaced the remains of the fallen city of Jerusalem with a Roman colony and renamed it *Aelia Capitolina*. A temple to Jupiter (Zeus) was placed at the site of the former Jewish temple and another temple platform was erected over the site of the rock quarry. Its temple was dedicated to Venus (Aphrodite), the goddess of love. The site of the tomb and crucifixion was built over and covered only about 100 years after the Resurrection.

With the rise in status of the Christian faith came an official recognition of religio licita, making it a legitimate legal religion in the Empire. By 326CE, Helena, the mother of the emperor Constantine, journeyed to Jerusalem and sought out the place of Jesus' death and resurrection. Local memory was strong enough to convince Helena that the original site was under the temple platform to the goddess Venus, despite the fact that the site was now located within the city walls (and had been for nearly 300 years) and had been covered by the Venus shrine for nearly 200 years. A far less expensive site to build the church would have been slightly north, nearer to a suspected Forum site, where the construction could have been erected unhindered. Instead, a massive excavation was undertaken by Emperor Constantine, exposing the cemetery and hill of Golgotha. The latter was left open to the air in an area consequently named "the Holy Garden," while the former was isolated as a free-standing edicule by cutting around it into the cliff side. In 335 CE, a dedication of the first pilgrim church in the Holy Land, the *Martyrion*, was conducted at the building over the ancient quarry.

The *Martyrion* stood on the site until 614 CE, when the Persians burned many churches and shrines in the land. They partially destroyed the edifice, which was later rebuilt, but not to its original size or beauty. Though less in splendor, the function of the site as a place of Christian celebration and worship continued until 1009 CE, when Hakim (often referred to as "mad") the caliph of Cairo, waged a campaign to destroy Christian and Jewish holy sites. The *Martyrion* was left in ruins and the bedrock tomb remembering Jesus' conquering of death was chipped down to its foundations.

Constantine IX Monomachus, between 1042 and 1048 CE, after becoming the Byzantine emperor, supported a program to rebuild and renovate the church. This fresh work on the edifice increased its size to roughly that of the church today. Nevertheless it was only about half of the splendor of its predecessor.

With the arrival of the Crusaders in 1099 CE and their efforts to "reclaim" the church, the structure was given its current arrangement of chapels, changing the formerly eastern main entrance to a southern main entrance and covering the rock of Golgotha with a building.

Evidences indicating the legitimacy of the site of the Church of the Holy Sepulchre

Most scholars point first to the evidence of location to indicate the veracity of the memory of the place: Topographical considerations, those being the line of the Transversal Valley running east from Jaffa Gate to the Temple Mount, and the eastern side of the quarry, as well as archeological considerations, the major one being the remains of a wall under the neighboring Redeemer Church, indicate that the site was outside of the Second Wall, which would have been the northern city limit in Jesus' day (the execution takes place outside the city, Matthew 27:32 and John 19:17). Golgotha would then be in full view of the city ramparts, highlighting the primary reason for Roman use of crucifixion as a punishment – deterrence.

A second, and very important evidence is found in pilgrim memory, collectively people recalled this event because it was so central to their faith. Found in the present lower Armenian Chapel of St. Krikor, there is a now faith charcoal drawing of a boat with an inscription underneath it: *"DOMINE IVIMUS"* ("Lord, we shall go," reference to Ps. 122:1). After intense study, it has been marked as the earliest known Christian pilgrim graffiti in the Holy Land. The use of Latin indicates that the artist probably came from North Africa or Europe. Its value is in its pre-Constantine date, which points to a longer, and therefore more reliable, tradition on which to base authenticity. Further, no other site was considered as the possible location until 1883.

All other evidences would be muted if there were no existing *Kokhim* style tomb remains found in the place, since that is the style of any "new tomb" cut from rock in the period. Though little other than some bedrock remains on the revered tomb site, there are other Herodian period tombs still existing within the church. This is a likely indication of burial at this site in the age of Jesus (Matthew 27:60, Luke 23:53, and John 19:41).

The Value of the Remembrance

For Christian pilgrims and travelers who visit the Holy Land, but are not from a liturgical background, it is often difficult to understand the motivation behind and the benefit of remembrances like the stations of the Via Dolorosa and the chapels of the Holy Sepulchre. Some Protestant groups who come to the land express that have little or no desire to recall "tradition" such as the one that the Via Dolorosa embraces.

There is a definite value, however, to be found in the gift given to the Christian pilgrim by the Franciscans in the establishment and maintenance of the reflective walk that takes place each Friday. Even stations that were not a part of the Biblical account have carefully considered reasons as to why they are now included in the walk.

The first two stations come directly from the pages of the New Testament. Jesus was condemned to death by Pontius Pilate and given a cross (probably only the crossbeam, called the *patibulum*) to carry as a condemned prisoner (John 19:16). Recalling the sufferings of Jesus as the Bible offers them is always of value.

The third station, "Jesus fell," like that of the seventh and ninth, helps us to focus on the humanity of Jesus and His frailty as an exhausted man. In a climate that has so theologized the Savior, it is certainly valuable to remind ourselves that God "became flesh, and dwelt among us," as the Gospel writer encourages.

By the fourth station, we find ourselves remembering the terror of viewing the beaten and tortured Christ as Mary would have seen Him. Today we can find women standing nearby the memory place, some with tear filled eyes, that have come to seek a compassionate warmth from God because they too have suffered the loss of a loved one. The station reminds us that the Savior endured pain for us, but those closest to him suffered as well. The presence of Mary and john at the cross are New Testament memories of this as well.

The inclusion of Simon of Cyrene at the fifth station, in addition to the fact the Biblical writer includes the story in the detail of the journey, is helpful because it pulls into the story a marginal person, a bystander (Luke 23:26). Even those not trying to be a part of the story are drawn into the sufferings of Jesus. One man, far from his home and people, would forever be changed by this encounter.

The sixth station draws into the story a woman who steps out into the path to wipe the face of Jesus. Why include this in the journey? It is helpful to remember that not everyone in the story is callused and uncaring. In the Veronica tradition, we see the gentleness and care that otherwise seems lacking in the memory of the account. Some people cared. They may not have been the powerful, but they cared, and risked to show it.

In the eighth station, Jesus speaks about the coming terrible days of the city of Jerusalem and presents another aspect of His own character (Luke 23:28). In the midst of His own pain, His concern was for the coming suffering of others. The servant's heart described in the second and third chapters of Philippians is well depicted in such a scene.

The final stations recall Biblical scenes that are essential to the memory of the story. Having been awake much of the previous night, incarcerated, wrongly accused and mocked, Jesus arrived at the site of the execution exhausted. Beaten beyond belief, with His beard partially torn from His face, He lay down on the ground and had nails driven into His flesh.

The physical pain and sufferings of the Savior are an essential memory if the excitement and power of the Resurrection is to fill and stir the followers of Jesus even today.

The church of the Holy Sepulchre, while not infallibly so, is the best archeological candidate for the authentic site of the death and Resurrection of Jesus. Its long, continuous tradition attests to the validity of its memory. The site is distinguished not only as the site of these events, however, but as a site of pilgrimage throughout the ages.

The memory of pilgrims for generations, the symbols found in their gifts and offerings, and things as small as the writings of graffiti tell the real story of the site. The One that died on a tree so long ago was the One to whom each looked for help and care, for eternal salvation. Visitors to the site, though benefiting from the memory engendered by the geographical location, have always been encouraged to look among the living for evidences of the Risen Lord.

The Garden Tomb: Another Important Memory Place

Behind the East Jerusalem bus station, a rocky escarpment leaves the impression of a large skull, with eye sockets indenting the hillside above the idling buses. Inside the fenced area below is "The Garden Tomb" a property that attracts pilgrims from around the world who come to worship the Savior in a place that recalls the empty tomb and His powerful resurrection from the dead. It is at the heart of the Gospel, and as such the place draws worshipers of Jesus from cities spread around the globe.

The site includes a rock-cut tomb, cleared in 1867 and subsequently considered by some Christians (particularly Protestant ones) to be a likely site for the burial and resurrection of Jesus of Nazareth. Proposed as a Biblical site since the mid-nineteenth century, Biblical scholars saw a correlation between the New Testament description of Golgotha (or "Skull Hill") and the look of the escarpment. The place has been maintained as a "holy site" since 1894, when a Christian non-denominational charitable trust based in the United Kingdom took over the property.

The Gospels clearly placed the crucifixion outside the walled city of Jerusalem, but very nearby. Throughout the Middle Ages, some pilgrims expressed dismay when they discovered the place of the Church of the Holy Sepulchre appeared to be very much inside the ancient walls of the city.

The controversy continued for generations. One later German pilgrim named Jonas Korte wrote in 1743: "On Mount Calvary, which now lies in the middle of the town and cannot therefore be the true Calvary". By 1841, Dr. Edward Robinson, the Dean of Union Theological Seminary in New York and one of the world's most renowned scholars in the Gospel and Koine Greek published his "Biblical Researches in Palestine", a reference work on the topography and archaeology of the Holy Land. Robinson concluded: "Golgotha and the Tomb shown in the Church of the Holy Sepulchre are not upon the real places of the Crucifixion and Resurrection" because he speculated the Church of the Holy Sepulchre location would have been within the city walls, based upon visual and topographical considerations. (It is worth noting that contemporary scholars, such as Professor Dan Bahat and Professor Gabriel Barkay (the author's former professor) have concluded that the Church of the Holy Sepulchre was located well outside the city walls in the days of Jesus and therefore can no longer be ruled out as a possible location for the crucifixion and burial of Jesus.)

The theory of the Garden Tomb as the actual location was advanced by a number of important writings and scholar. Claude R. Conder in <u>Tent Work in Palestine: A Record of Discovery and Adventure</u>, Vol. I (London, 1878), p. 327 argued, that the Church of the Holy Sepulchre was in an improper location (within the walls) and proposed the site the Garden Tomb Association now displays. The place was again endorsed by Major-General Charles Gordon who visited Jerusalem in 1883. Later news articles attributed the "discovery" to Gordon, though it was not really his at all. So called "Gordon's Calvary" should have been given a different name.

Climbing into the tomb, several important observations can be made. First, it is part of a larger tomb complex that can be seen on the opposite side of the rock in the adjacent property – this was the place of a First Temple Period cemetery. Second, this site yields a two-chambered rock cut structure. The style of the interior was typical of the 8th century BCE, and did not conform to the "kochim" style tomb that a "new tomb" from the time of Jesus should exhibit. The earliest detailed investigation of the tomb appears to have been from a report of Conrad Schick (1874). A very thorough re-investigation was made a century later Dr. Gabriel Barkay, professor of Biblical archaeology at the Hebrew University of Jerusalem and Bar-Ilan University.

The Value of the Garden Tomb

Since we established that the Via Dolorosa contained "memory sites" that were made for places of prayer, Scripture contemplation and reflection, we can apply the same thoughts to the Garden Tomb. The archaeology points elsewhere, but the Garden nevertheless beckons. Since the point of Jesus' coming was not to change the rocks – but rather the lives of people – we sit in the garden to hear the songs of the nations, believers in Jesus who converge on this garden and raise their voices in praise to Jesus Christ, Who changed them by His love. To them, there is no question of the value of the place. It is here they can sense the love of Jesus, and His powerful resurrection is recalled time and again.

Made in the USA
Columbia, SC
21 September 2023

23161993R00020